AF484628

Young Thing

Poems by
Grace Bialecki

Photos by
Alex Brook Lynn

RAINBOW
SKULL

This book is published by Rainbow Skull.
www.rainbowskull.xyz
"Only connect!"

ISBN (trade paperback) 979-8-9926666-2-5
ISBN (ebook) 979-8-9926666-3-2

First Edition: September 2025

"...But anything worth doing is

worth doing badly."

– "Failing and Flying" by Jack Gilbert

Contents

Early Aughts

Some days, my mid-thirties are so oppressive. Make me miss American Apparel, iced soy chais, and my sports coaches before consent was invented. Still want Leo, Brad, and Johnny to be smoldering, un-cancellable. That golden era when each divine female was anorexia-inspiring, when we paid tithes in shed pounds, when Cosmopolitan was our Bible, preaching sex positions that would be recompensed. All the requisite contortions for future husbands. Walk the path of miniskirts and ruched dresses, hems riding up and up, as we strode into the bar with nothing to offer other than our underaged allure. *All we have to do is stand here,* my pretty, skinny friend said while the men bought us everything. What was there to fear? All bones and hard liquor, I never remembered my nightmares.

Just Can't Get Enough

My first trip we responsibly decided His Best Friend would drive us back across LA. He'd only taken one hit and sobriety was a construct anyway. The One True and I melted in the backseat while Fergie's voice fused into us. That summer *Just Can't Get Enough* wouldn't stop playing. Its synthetic hook mixed with the neon sprawl as we soared to the liquor store then materialized in Venice. Drank whiskey straight until my brain short circuited. Rebooting the next morning, His Best Friend's mother mistook me for The One True's real girlfriend, which again I dreamed to be, instead of an acid side-piece. Nineteen, that first trip stuck like a pop song — *addicted and I just can't get enough* — before it became insipid through years of repet-repet-repet-repetition.

Inception

How to remember the beginning when those were the years we drank into oblivion? From the poolside where they discovered me to that graduation rager. His Best Friend's bravado, and The One True's sullen genius. Aura broken, yet fixable. My naivety fathomless. Something about the crack in his voice when he said my name. That rasp that latched onto my brain. His uniform of white t-shirts. We were both too brilliant for that prestigious oasis where we de-constructed on a daily basis. Spurning the library to write in Adderall-fueled flurries. Unlike the couples canoodling from carrel to dining hall — soon to be spawning more liberal elites — we didn't believe in monogamy. Mashed our bodies blacked-out on Oxy. Innovating. Obfuscating. The stickiness of all that sex, kush, and collusion. So years later, he still sneaks into my stories. Except I'm ready to delete them all off my laptop. That page I never expected where The One True told me that one night when I was *all fucked up,* I reached for his hand. And that's how we began.

**Only Time I've Ever
Been**

Went to the Hamptons and
fought with The Musician.
Took photos on the beach,
masking our dysfunction.
My new white suit instantly
dingy. Back at the mansion,
encountered a woman in a
hammock whose husband
was my former paramour.
Pawing at the cobwebs of
my mistress era while the
spiders and socialites crept
a c r o s s t h e l a w n .
Abandoned beer pong and
left The Musician to lose
alone. I drank and drank
and drank. Mirror-selfie in
the bathroom with the
opulent avian wallpaper
then stumbled into a
stranger. *Oh,* he said,
brightening. *You're a pretty
young thing.*

Groupie

Did I mention The Musician drew tears merely by bowing his violin? Wrists stiff with tendonitis from coercing notes so pure. He got almost-famous in an indie band, and I was there from basement show to his face on the Jumbotron — who could've ignored those cheekbones? Back then I lurked, flushing and mumbling whenever The Lead Singer asked, *So what do you do?* The Musician would intervene — *She's in a band, too*, though I did nothing other than leech his glory, incite dissonant spats, and let him play me so well. It's been ten years, and when I listen to his music, I'm maudlin, awash in deceitful melodies. Ready to reprise my role, stoned and alone at his band's reunion show. The Lead Singer recognizes me — no longer blonde or demur, but still in my place facing the stage. While The Musician is out making it in LA. Replaced by some weak-ass viola. Text him a video. No response. Only aching harmonies that fade with the final chord.

Oh, the ego

who loved waking up next to The Musician and seeing a text from The One True. *I miss you.* Even wrote my name, too. No comma, no period. But I forgave his punctuation. Forgave the months of silence, decreed by his latest girlfriend. Forgave the way he'd announced her via email. Now he was the one missing me. Texting, confessing. How enticing to take him back twice. To call it fate instead of the same mistake.

Petty

And so we arrived in that spiteful winter when I stood glittered, blowing breath clouds outside the bodega on Bedford Ave. The Musician exited with a six-pack, proceeded to dump me. (I wasn't even being bitchy!) Savage-brained and icy, unable to walk home alone in my furry hat, I wrapped his words around my fingers and lured him back to bed. Needed more months in our cave, gnashing my teeth and performing intimacy. When really, I was waiting to gnaw my way out, profess my love for The One True, and reclaim this tiny life as mine to reign and ruin.

Family Vacation

En route to Africa, The One True's mother passed out Ambien like after-dinner mints. Horny and sedated, I proceeded to paw her son beneath an airplane blanket. There was a way, I thought, as I drifted off, to slide on top and consummate our eternal love. Later, he would call it misguided — my invitation, the entire family vacation — but there on Royal Air Maroc, I contorted my nubile limbs, ready to defy geometry for him.

Editorializing Bacon

It started with the photo of her puppy paws on his bare chest — The One True's first pet. Sure, he was co-parenting with His Best Friend, but what marked adulthood more than dog dads? Promenading her down the boardwalk and spoiling her on fatty meats. She got UTIs from rubbing her doggy vag in the beach grass, and The One True took her straight to the vet, proving his ability to care and repair. He didn't use less, but thumbed any white speck in an attempt at vigilance. It was easy for me to coo from a distance, though when I arrived with my duffel, she would eye me — drooly and distrusting — then plop down in the middle of his bed. Immovable. So The One True bent me around the bulldog at acute angles. So good at sex, it had to be all his practice. Mattress's sighs confessing the other trysts. That year for his birthday, his colleagues procured a thick cake with the dog's portrait, somehow edible. More pawing, more nuzzles filling the chasm of his childhood. Yes, I spent years editorializing Bacon. Writing an asthmatic bulldog into the role of savior. Expecting her to trot the plot toward happily ever after, instead of slobbering through her father's decay.

Love Sex Dreams

Our second trip, we responsibly decided not to drive. It was just us in the countryside, and I couldn't stop seeing flocks of peacocks. Had The One True bite my arm, hard. His teeth comfort amidst the chaos we'd created — time and other facades eviscerated. So when I descended the stairs my limbs became a Cubist experiment. And as I reached for The One True, silver flickered through his hair. It was all so clear: we would reassemble and grow old together. These melting hours a portent, our fate sealed when The One True kissed me, and it tasted like coming home. Whiskey, weed, and the same spit I'd always known. Somehow we shed our clothes and made love under the stars like dirty hippies. Our souls tripping in a realm of pure bliss, above the plane of doubt or pain. Scientifically speaking, the acid etched our love into my brain.

Remember Our Hair?

For years the drugs only made him hotter, a battered rock star. He didn't talk more, only cynical asides in that rasp that dropped straight to my pussy. Those pale eyes that tore through me. Sometimes I watched as women oozed around, seduced by him doing nothing. But I was the one who'd been there when he had short hair, no scruff, studying economics and reading David Foster Wallace. I was the one he emailed, parents cced, re: Family Vacation.

Once he even drove me to LAX. Freshman year, unclear how we'd conceived this agreement. The One True was venomous that morning, hissing when I ripped open his curtains, so I retreated and packed him the bong. He came in quiet then ran his hand across my bare back and through my hair. All splintered and blonde. The longest it's ever been.

Survival Instincts

I wrote tragic poetry. Biked to work every day, no subways, in the mean rain. Needed those gritty miles to blow the indignities of my office job off me. I went to yoga and learned to breathe. It wasn't easy. Then finally, I had a sliver of clarity wide enough to look back and see The Musician with his unflinching vision. And I knew I too needed an art, needed an anything, to save me from myself.

Poem About What Never Happened

We have the conversation about my needs, and he agrees. Stops swilling Oxy and fucking his way to happy. His shrink and psychiatrist dial down the depression. He keeps meditating, walking Bacon. Quits smoking. Business booms, and he opens that New York office. We arrive in our thirties, not as soft as those college couples, but leaning toward content. Teasing each other with a decade's worth of fodder. He doesn't liquify his brain into a drug slurry. His brilliant snark whizzes through the air, as he stays himself, The One True.

Five Stars

After I'd packed my bags, bought a flight back, and ended it all with The One True Ex, I took the most tragic Uber to LAX. But the driver had five-star banter. *You look like that singer,* he said, eyeing me in the rearview. *In that group.* We made it through Marina del Rey before we finally landed on Fergie. I look nothing like her, but the comparison was a soft rain on the barren expanse of my future. From Fergie we moved to fitness, and tips for my un-achievable pull-ups. I bathed myself in our exchange, as he drove me further and further from the hallucination of my longest relationship. Then we arrived at Terminal 3, and my driver turned to me. All brolic arms and body spray, locking eyes so I was already edging away as he threw his final pitch. *Driving isn't shit* — he was really a bodyguard for C-list celebrities. *Tell me, do you ever need personal protection?*

All the time, I thought. *All the fucking time.*

The Word No One Would Say

Horseshit, The One True Ex hissed. *Horseshit.* The last word he spit at me. He and His Best Friend were on the phone — of course I couldn't get them alone — and I was fighting my final battle. *Danger zone. Overdose. Rehab.* Had even called for a drug test, but it came back clean. The lie so blatant, I never asked for an explanation. They were feral in California while I dry-heaved at my red Formica table, a Craigslist treasure I'd hauled from Greenpoint. Manhandling my dreams down city blocks and up tight stairwells. *Horseshit.* And that was the end of it. No heartfelt letters, no family meetings, no therapist's checklist. Kept expecting it to go like on the TV show, but I never watched a single episode, so what did I know? All I had was a primal need to intervene. My feminine tenacity ready to match The One True Ex's impending wrath. As I shot back that unspeakable word: *Addict.*

Addict.

Addict.

SONIA RYKIEL

Une étrangère

Je pense que tu es une étrangère, said The Future French Husband as he slid in next to me. What a relief to have a body filling that seat. One who spoke in tidy sentences, not a drunken blend of slang and *verlan* that tripped my tongue. I'd put nine time zones between myself and The One True Ex — betting on this moment. While once I'd been drunk and witty, now all I had was my stilted vocabulary. *Néanmoins*, The Future French Husband carried on gallantly. He was older, drove a moto, and had me write my info on a scrap of paper. The formality, the chivalry. When all I wanted was a native who would take me to galleries and never touch LSD. And so our romance unfolded like a months-long high school dialogue. Even impressed myself by the way I learned to yell. *Je m'en fiche. Je m'en fous. Tu es rigide. Tu es impossible.* But The Future French Husband was right about one thing: I was an *étrangère*, a stranger and a foreigner, and I'd stay that way until the day we parted.

Moins Jolie

Let's blame Colette, or actually Kiera who played her in the biopic. Careening through Paris, writing scandals in her pantsuit and shorn curls. *Bien sûr*, I took my same ambitions to the coiffeur. *Un coup à la garçonne?* The owner verified, eyeing. Neither she nor The French Husband thought I would dare. *Tu serais moins jolie,* he'd said to me. As if that shoulder-length straw was my most laudable feature. *Je suis jolie à l'interieur.* But my counter-attack was futile against the citadel of his normativity. The coiffeur started with a rough hack, each falling lock freedom. Though I didn't know that I was cutting off The French Husband. Soon my resistance clashed with his barricades: brooding distance, lack of caresses, The French Husband not even touching my tresses. Surely Colette would've plotted an exuberant escape, but it took me months to make my break. My medicines, my money, my novels were all tied to that man — without him I was just another queer American. Stumbling through the city of beauty and patriarchy, *moins jolie*, but finally me.

Plan à Trois

Months after I left him, I still remembered The Former French Husband's history lesson given from his moto. *Picasso, Gide, la résistance et l'occupation*, inevitably ending in the gutting of Hôtel Lutetia. Later, chauffeurless, I returned via the 86 bus. Frigid night. City lights. My Parisian life, and its textbook reckless behavior sashaying into the place The Former French Husband so disdained. Now gaudy, nouveau luxury, ravaged by rich tourists. Yes, I let them fuck me. The wife mostly, while the husband played with himself in the corner. Both their photos false advertising, but mine didn't lie — *you're so tiny*, she yelped as she stripped me bare. Orgasms, then the imperative cigarette. Possessions triple-checked, I made my exit. Sole set of footsteps in the marble lobby, promiscuity wafting off me, as I fingered my cab money and told the concierge to call one in my silkiest French. My therapist would have had a field day with all of this, so of course, I never told her.

Visitation

In the dream, The One True Ex is all shiny eyes and wolfish smile. Lounging in his requisite white T and offering unsolicited commentary about the album I put on. These minor skirmishes our easiest way of flirting. Isn't it lovely to hear him opine? To share that time, even if it never happens.

The Key to Happiness

Second date, I played all my cards and invited her to the oyster
bar. But they were creamy, *les huîtres lactées*, lactating even.
This didn't stymie my seduction — flashed black mesh under
my blazer and impressed my lover with my vocabulary,
specifically the word *résille*. Fishnet. Of course, The Former
French Husband had taught me this. *Résille*. A staple of my
wardrobe. As the evening unfolded from bivalves and Chablis
into foreplay, all of this revelry incited a lurking migraine,
which despite our best efforts, I couldn't come my way out of.
So what I really remember about that night is my lover's
assessment given while I nodded dully, temples crawling:
there was a man on Rue Saint-Anne who must massage my
scalp. 300€ an hour. There was a muscle that ran from my
skull into my neck, and as long as it was tense, I would never
be happy.

J'ai Faim

Today I am hungry for more than poetry and peanut butter. An apple cleaved through the core. Half a banana mashed onto toast. Flakes of a fish fillet. Raised in an era of double zeros, so my brain blinks at the new ads with those models who are cavorting, flaunting, instead of folding themselves. Cucumber. Cubed watermelon. Lemon water. Chiseling myself smaller. *You've got some track laid wrong,* my therapist says. As if we're blaming a locomotive company whose brawny men hammered stakes into my brain. Soup bowl of popcorn. Almond milk. Another spoonful of some butter.

But when the Parisian doctors asked my weight, I could never internalize the conversion. *Cinquante? Peut-être cinquante-cinq?* They'd make their little scoff of disbelief and herd me onto the scale. Proclaim another number that finally had no meaning. Then end the exam with hollow instructions: *Stérilet. Analyze de sang. À jeun.* I was already the bumbling American, bursting in with my oily skin, nearly vanquished by the courtyards and codes, the miscounted stories. Even after four years, I couldn't tell you what *trente-huit* means in waist or feet. If the second floor is actually the third.

Pourquoi as-tu osé de la quitter?

Sometimes I wonder how I left her in all her preening, antiquated splendor. Bless the cantankerous *hommes d'affaires* battling for the sanctity of her cobblestones. Each strike of my battered boots echoing their praise. Each spring, the plane trees raining their pollen down on the boulevards. Those haughty diagonals only ever leading to the vainglorious *rond points et étoiles,* a city of pompous, impossible intersections. Each cemetery walk wet and gothic. The ghosts closer on those mossy tombs, and the one bench with the view I could only find when lost. Each cigarette that wafted across. The smoker's burnt clouds mixing with coffee and croissants. Each morning, pedaling the river's quays to the library then treading worn stone steps into strict silence. How could I dare be miserable when I got exactly what I wanted? Leather tomes and stoic table lamps. A dark-haired man who wove his moto through traffic, always cursing *les embouteillages dans ce bordel de merde.* Promised to buy me a matching helmet, but I clambered aboard long before I realized it was a lie. Each summer's flawless sky. That electric possibility coursing through the city, crackling from evening into night, the wine crisp, endless, no one ever speaking of sleeping. Each time I tangled up those streets and still promised myself I would never leave.

Another Poem That Ends at LAX

but begins at Starbucks on Santa Monica Boulevard where
His Best Friend agreed to meet before my flight. Even
offered me a ride, though I didn't trust the gesture until he
arrived — six years more battered, but capable of a coffee
date. First topic is my hair, from there, the only two
creatures we ever speak of: Bacon has cancer. The One
True Ex can't keep track of her pills. He's even less
functional than when we tried to send him to rehab. A
mutual failing, though I was burned as the witch. The
meddling bitch from the East. I'm cradling my jasmine tea
when His Best Friend drops the bomb on me. *I took that
drug test for him. I peed in the cup.* The waves of traffic, the
LA haze, every proper response evades my brain. I don't
throw my scalding drink in his useless face. Don't blister
guilt into his betrayal. Because didn't I orchestrate this
absurd reunion? So at Starbucks, I'm all soft words and
sighs, and soon we're driving down the 405, arriving at that
haunted terminal. And I want to acknowledge how we've
both lost our One True, but all I can do is gather my bags.
And His Best Friend doesn't get out of his pick-up, doesn't
even unbuckle his seatbelt, so when I heave across to hug
him, it's all elbows.

Waiting for The Thoughts To Stop Being Thought

Waiting for His Best Friend's wedding, and the drama of that seating chart. Waiting for the phone call about The One True Ex's funeral. Waiting for The Musician to drop the album that makes me cry, cry, cry. Waiting for The Former French Husband to be less fucking French. Waiting for my therapist to stop texting me videos about narcissists. Waiting for my twenties to crinkle and crease, folded by my hands into poems.

Trying

Paid full-price for the emotional release workshop and barely shed a tear. Just huffed the beery carpet and groveled in the supine posture, supplicating as demonstrated. Nothing. The music's bullshit lyrics were distracting, and what we were doing in that warehouse under the trestle bridge, hard up against the sketchy inlet? The space was for raves, which seemed more cathartic than this bawling and thrashing. The others heaving and wailing while I doubted I'd ever emit such a sound. Already imagining the relief of emerging from this turmoil and smoking something under the fat moon. Just us and our fathomless secrets. It wasn't until phase three — integration — the music still cheesy, everyone weaving, that I pressed my forehead into the wall and the tears began to fall. Instead of all my heartbreakers, I saw that gray mare circling the arena. No halter or lunge line. And all I'd do was say *whoa* and shift my feet, and she'd hop to a stop. Ears pricked, and her darling eyes asking, *I did it right, right?*

Look At Me Now

At The Lead Singer's apartment, I'm no longer a groupie. An artist, finally, assembling my sax and confessing, *I don't know how to do that.* She soothingly corrects: *I don't know how to do that, yet.* Yet, somehow I do. In minutes, I build a soundscape of my own tortured interior. Primitive compared to The Musician's exquisite creations. But it's mine. All mine. Wonder if I could've made him the backing track, so the spotlight shone on my poems. No. One of us had to be more famous. More blameless. One had to be more wily. The other, beguiling. One had to run faster. One had to mop up our disasters. And this afternoon I am older than all those power struggles. Bike across the bridge sweating my face off. Sax strapped to my back. How many years of coming home to no one did it take until I was the one I loved?

In Memoriam

Today I miss all my old cats. The saintly tabby taken by leukemia who sat with me through my adolescence. His amber eyes and infinite patience as I read trashy paperbacks. I miss the feral black and white one who scratched me capriciously. Didn't come inside until a decade of winters wore her tame. By then she was bird-boned, badgered by the splotchy rogue kitten we rescued from a decrepit shed. That young thing reigned alone, doted on, until my father's new wife sent her to a farm. Or so the saying goes. For all my years of meditations, I still haven't forgiven that treason. I miss my uncle's sickly purebred, another gentle angel, who slept inches from my face. Filled my days with pills and tiny syringes, fighting the illness that rotted his fur. I miss my ornery gray tabby who's still alive. Gave her away three times, and now she lives in Brooklyn. Yowls every visit. I was nineteen when I found her on Craigslist. Unable to care for anything including myself. I still cry best in the shower, wet snot shooting straight down. Catless and itinerant, I pay hundreds a month to hug a rich lady's dappled mare. Braid her mane, shovel her shit. In the pasture with her steadfast presence, the chaos of my every romance is abundantly clear. All I can do is hang her halter, drive myself back, and talk with my old cats.

Manifest Destiny

Lately I want to go somewhere none of this happened. No break-up bodegas, sticky concert halls, no tearful airport terminals. I want terra incognita instead of that taco truck on Sepulveda whose horchata is a sweet hangover. I want a city free of bulldogs, so I don't encounter Bacon on the corner. How did she, spoiled on Philly cheesesteaks, not outlive The One True Ex and all his self-poisoning? In-bred, a creature-like canine always snorty and snuffling. He loved her more than me. Easier to accept than the betrayal of him loving the pills, maybe more than both of us. Give me freedom from the tortured cities of my twenties. No more bar stools and thick Bloody Marys. Never re-enter that café where I waited tables and closed out cash drawers. Always off in a way no amount of re-counting could change. Leave all those obsolete nickels and pennies. Erase the faces of the cranky hippies who I served Genmaicha Tea. Never correcting when they called it roasted barley.

It's time to erase myself from this place. Time to reclaim my lampshades. My grandmother's steamer trunk. Wrap up my gaudy teapot. My books are already cuddling in boxes — I've been death cleaning my whole life — and now I'll drive until I disappear. My tiny, aggressively bumper-stickered car proclaiming *Namasté, bitches* the entire way. Put miles of highway between me and the psychos haunting my poems. Exhale anonymity. Let me be just another legging-wearing white woman in a state where no one cares about repairing their face. Where the billboards switch from God to marijuana. Where it's too expensive to tear down those gorgeous ruined warehouses. Another river, another island, but no damn people. Solitude. And the glory of those flat summer sunsets that just keep on going. Yes, I'll drive west and settle someplace only my best ghosts know.

Gratitude

This collection wouldn't exist if I hadn't begun practicing meditation, studying Buddhism, and observing my thought loops and conditioning. Thank you to my teachers and guides along this path — especially Peter Doobinin, Linda Erman, and the women in Mindfulness Meditation Teacher Certification and my Detroit practice circle.

Even with a collection of this length, a writer needs feedback and support. These poems would never have reached their truest forms without the months of help from EK Bartlett. Thank you to the other writers and friends who read this manuscript and encouraged me along the way: Ronny Kerr, Annie Hennessy, Matt Jones, Katie Lazaro, Eléonore Mahée, and Ashna Ali.

A special thank you to my poetic heroine, Diane Seuss, who inspires me to write past the end of my poems and let them decide where to go.

Gratitude to my dear friend and collaborator, Alex Brook Lynn. Of course you would have photos waiting from Los Angeles, New York, and Paris. It's a joy to make art with you and have ours together in this book.

To Joe Gallagher from Rainbow Skull. Thank you for getting it, and for all your work and thought that turned this collection into a book.

Appreciation to my family who have always supported my artistic endeavors. And to my students, young and old, who inspire me with their ideas and questions, and who remind me to follow my own advice.

Thank you to the staff and security guards of the Sojourner Truth Library and Detroit Public Library where this collection was written and edited. Without you, I wouldn't have a space to write, contemplate, and create.

About the Author

Grace Bialecki is a writer, meditation teacher, and workshop facilitator who inspires artists to be present in their lives and with the work. She has taught hundreds of workshops for organizations from Hugo House to Detroit Horse Power to the Brooklyn Public Schools. Her writing has appeared in various publications including The Millions, Catapult, and Epiphany Magazine where she was a monthly columnist. Grace has performed her poetry in Detroit, Paris, and at New York's KGB Bar and Salmagundi Club. She is the co-founder of the storytelling series *Thirst,* and the author of the novella *Purple Gold* (ANTIBOOKCLUB). For more, visit: www.graciebialecki.com